MOON

Lynn M. Stone

Rourke
Publishing LLC
Vero Beach, Florida 32964

www.rourkepublishing.com

PHOTO CREDITS: Title page: © Alexey Stiop; page 4: © pinobarile; page 5: © NASA; page 6: © Sebastian Kaulitzki; page 7: © Mehmet Salih Guler; page 8: © Clint Spencer; page 9: © Michael Brake; page 10: © Varina and Jay Patel; page 11: © NASA; page 12: © NASA; page 13: © NASA; page 14: © Lynn Stone; page 15: © Johnny Lye; page 16: © NASA; page 17: © Ufuk ZIVANA, NASA; page 18-22: © NASA

Editor: Meg Greve

Cover and Interior designed by: Tara Raymo

Library of Congress Cataloging-in-Publication Data

Stone, Lynn M.
  Moon / Lynn Stone.
     p. cm. -- (Skywatch)
  Includes index.
  ISBN 978-1-60472-294-9
  1. Moon--Juvenile literature. I. Title.
  QB582.S76 2009
  523.3--dc22
                          2008024849

Printed in the USA

CG/CG

TABLE OF CONTENTS

THE MOON

The Moon is a big, ball-shaped object in outer space. It is Earth's closest neighbor in the **solar system**, yet it is still about 238,857 miles (384,403 kilometers) from the Earth. That is about the same distance as 10 trips around the widest part of planet Earth.

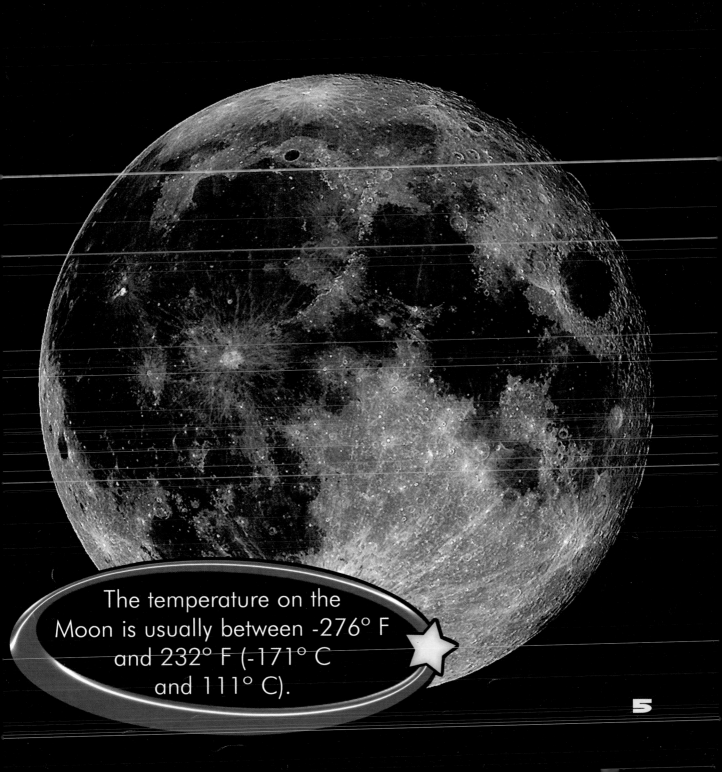

The temperature on the Moon is usually between -276° F and 232° F (-171° C and 111° C).

All of the objects in our solar system travel around the Sun in paths called **orbits**. **Planets** orbit the Sun, while the Moon orbits the Earth.

Because the Moon is rotating while it is orbiting the Earth, we always see the same side of the moon.

A powerful, pulling force from Earth called gravity keeps the Moon in its orbit. The Moon has its own gravity, but it is less powerful.

The pull of gravity from the Moon and Sun causes the oceans' tides.

9

THE MOON AND EARTH

The Moon is very different from the Earth.
The Moon does not have air, liquid water,
or life of its own.

The Moon is about 80 times smaller than the Earth.

The Moon is rocky and dusty. Mountains, valleys, and **craters** cover its surface. The craters at the Moon's **poles** contain ice.

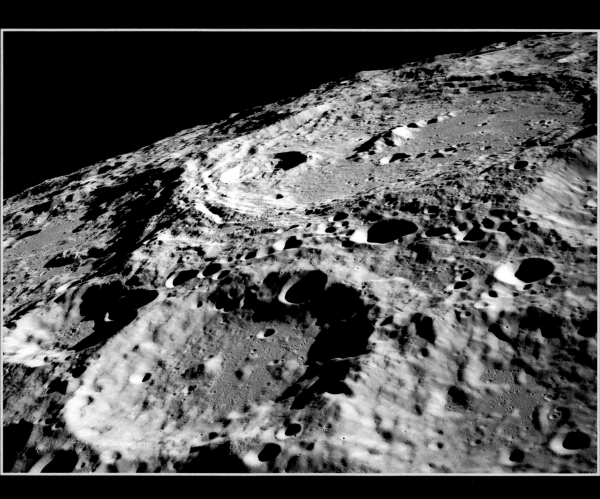

Scientists believe the craters on the Moon were formed by meteor crashes.

MOONLIGHT

During the period called a full Moon, the Moon looks like a big, bright ball. Moonlight is actually sunlight **reflecting** off the Moon's surface.

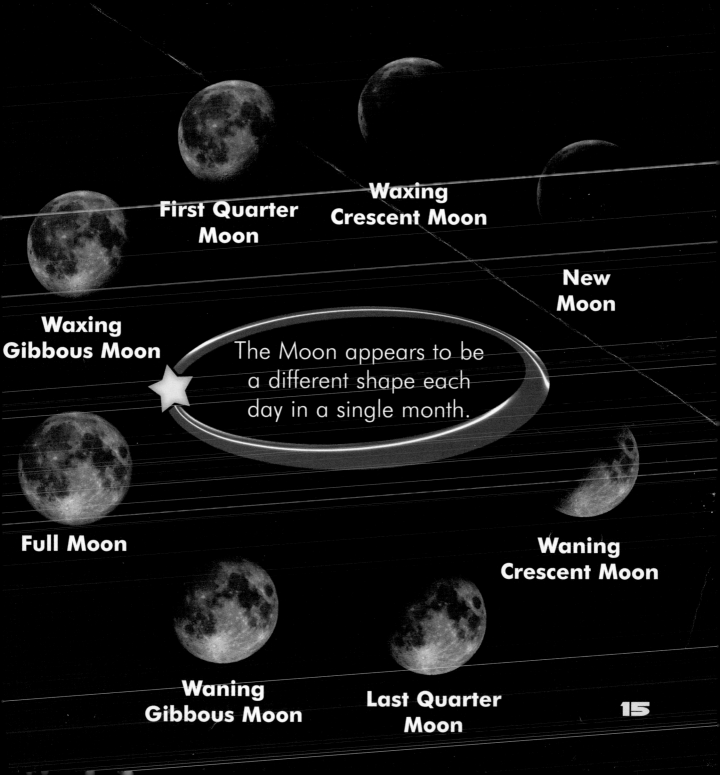

First Quarter Moon

Waxing Crescent Moon

New Moon

Waxing Gibbous Moon

The Moon appears to be a different shape each day in a single month.

Full Moon

Waning Crescent Moon

Waning Gibbous Moon

Last Quarter Moon

When the Sun, Earth, and Moon are in a line, the Earth's shadow blocks the Sun's light from the Moon. We call this a **lunar** eclipse.

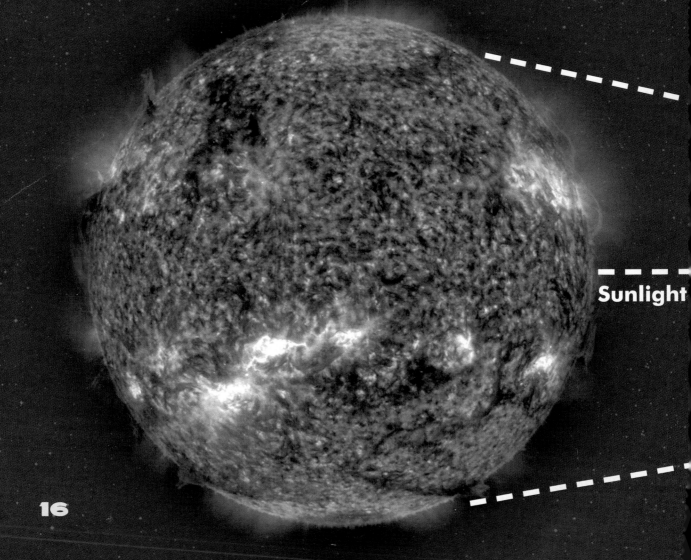

Sunlight

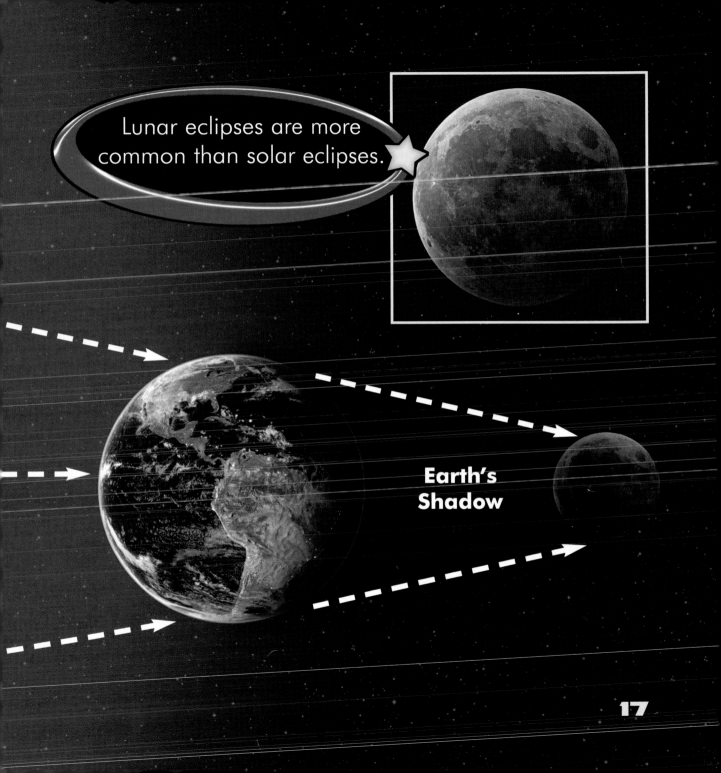

Lunar eclipses are more common than solar eclipses.

Earth's Shadow

ASTRONAUTS ON THE MOON

Between 1969 and 1972, several American **astronauts** walked on the Moon. Neil Armstrong was the first person to step onto the Moon's surface.

The American flag does not mean America owns the Moon. No country is allowed to own the Moon, stars, or other planets in outer space.

The astronauts had to bring everything they needed, including air, for their visits to the Moon.

Astronauts wore special suits with their own air supply.

Scientists hope that one day we can visit the Moon again. Maybe it will be you!

The new Ares I rocket might send people back to the Moon by 2020.

GLOSSARY

astronauts (ASS-truh-nawts): those who fly into higher altitudes, often into outer space

craters (KRAY-turs): holes or depressions on the Moon's surface

orbits (OR-bits): moves around another object in a circular path

poles (POLES): the two points farthest away from the middle

lunar (LOO-nur): to do with the Moon

planets (PLAN-its): several huge, ball-shaped objects in outer space that travel around the Sun

reflecting (ri-FLEKT-ing): bouncing off of another object

solar system (SOH-lur SISS-tuhm): the Sun and those objects in space bound to it by gravity

INDEX

FURTHER READING

Bingham, Caroline. *First Space Encyclopedia*. DK Publishing, 2008.

Kerrod, Robin. *Moon*. Lerner, 2003.

Twist, Clint. *The Moon*. School Specialty Publishing, 2006.

WEBSITES TO VISIT

http://www.frontiernet.net~kidpower/astronomy.html

www.kidsastronomy.com/earth/Moons.html

www.content.scholastic.com/browse/article.jsp?id=4850

ABOUT THE AUTHOR

Lynn M. Stone is a widely-published wildlife and domestic animal photographer and the author of more than 500 children's books. His book *Box Turtles* was chosen as an Outstanding Science Trade Book and Selectors' Choice for 2008 by the Science Committee of the National Science Teachers' Association and the Children's Book Council.